DAVID CO

10
DAYS
BENJAMIN
FRANKLIN

ALADDIN PAPERBACKS

NEW YORK   LONDON   TORONTO   SYDNEY

❧ ALADDIN PAPERBACKS • An imprint of Simon & Schuster Children's Publishing Division • 1230 Avenue of the Americas, New York, NY 10020 • Text copyright © 2008 by David Colbert • All illustrations, woodcuts, and photographs courtesy of the Library of Congress. • All rights reserved, including the right of reproduction in whole or in part in any form. • ALADDIN PAPERBACKS and related logo are registered trademarks of Simon & Schuster, Inc. • Cover designed by Karin Paprocki • Interior designed by David Colbert • The text of this book was set in Perpetua. • Manufactured in the United States of America • First Aladdin Paperbacks edition September 2008 • 10 9 8 7 6 5 4 3 2 1 • Library of Congress Control Number 2008920647 • ISBN-13: 978-1-4169-6466-9 • ISBN-10: 1-4169-6446-0

CONTENTS

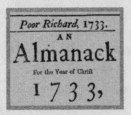

INTRODUCTION

Statesman, scientist, publisher, and popular author—Benjamin Franklin witnessed and shaped more events leading to independence than any other colonist. He represented the colonies in Britain. He signed the Declaration of Independence and the Constitution of the United States. He negotiated the treaty with France that helped win the Revolution, and the peace treaty with Great Britain that ended the war.

With just two years of traditional schooling, he became a celebrated philosopher and scientist. He discovered rules about electricity that are still taught today. Some of his many other scientific observations were more than a century ahead of their time.

Long before governments began to provide services to their citizens, he helped organize firefighters, schools, and a hospital.

His books were bestsellers. Some were translated and published across Europe. Lines he wrote are now common phrases.

He had remarkably few enemies for a man who played a part in creating a new, complex nation. When he made an enemy, there was usually a reason. By nature he was an optimist. He gave his trust generously and found that even difficult people gave him their trust in return.

He also had faults. He was obsessed with financial success and in business occasionally left people feeling misled. Though he preached often about avoiding vanity, at times his modesty was an act. His optimism sometimes blinded him to reality: He failed to understand for a long time that Britain's king, George III, would never give the colonists the rights they demanded. He was against slavery as an institution, but he owned slaves for a while and printed advertisements for slaves. For part of his life he held the usual prejudices against African Americans, slave or free. However, it must be said that he came around to the idea that "the black race" was "in every respect equal" to his own, which was a rare belief at the time, even among those people who wanted to end slavery.

He's an icon now, but he was a man once. He had his good days and his bad days, his boring days and his interesting days. He lived 30,761 days in all. Here are the ten that shook his world and yours.

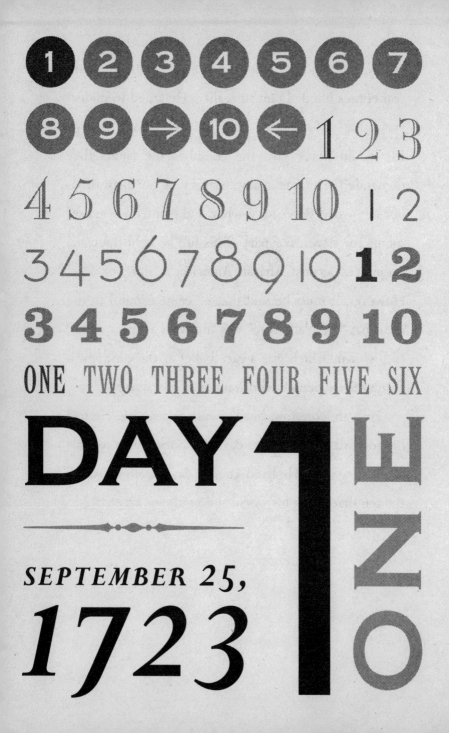

RUNAWAY

Boston. 6:12 P.M.

Tonight a teenage Ben Franklin is preparing his escape. Standing on a pier that stretches out into Boston Harbor, too nervous to notice the stench of warm fish guts, he's thinking back over the clumsy preparations he's made for his escape from the city. He still has to fool the captain of a ship sailing to New York tonight.

A few weeks ago Franklin was a great success. Just seventeen, he was the author of a popular newspaper column and was filling in as the newspaper's publisher. Now he's about to become a fugitive.

Worst of all, the person who would have him arrested on the spot is his brother.

REBELS WITHOUT A PAUSE

There's been trouble between Ben and his older brother James for a long time. For the last five years, Ben has been an apprentice in James's printing shop. James was reluctant to offer the position and Ben was reluctant to take it. Their father arranged it. By law, Ben has another four years of service left. He can't wait that long. He believes James wields his authority with too much force. That may be true. It's also true that Ben dislikes any authority.

Both brothers are born rebels, from a long line of them. In the 1500s, their ancestors in England were among the first Protestants, challenging the Roman Catholic Church. A later ancestor, a lawyer, helped commoners fight Britain's aristocracy. The name "Franklin" means "freeman," and Ben and James live up to it.

James is the only truly independent printer in Massachusetts. He's one of less than a handful in all of the colonies who's willing to criticize the government. His newspaper, the scandalous *New-England Courant*, makes a point of attacking the colony's leaders. James believes they're rigid, superstitious, and undemocratic.

His opinions are severe but reasonable. Some of his targets are the self-important churchmen who conducted the Salem witch trials. In that shameful affair, the government executed twenty so-called witches. As many as thirteen others died while in prison.

Ben and James are from a new generation. Boston has become an important seaport, and the trade with Europe brings ideas as well as goods. The town's church steeples are tall. The masts of the British East India Company's ships are taller.

BUTCHER, BAKER, CANDLESTICK MAKER?

en will eventually become so famous as a printer that it's easy to see his job with James as a natural choice. In fact he took it as a last resort.

When he's eight, Ben's enrolled at the South Grammar School. His father wants him to go to Harvard. The plan is for Ben to become a clergyman.

Ben does well at school. After his first year he skips a grade. Then, without warning, his father withdraws him. His father says the reason is that college would be too expensive. Historians aren't sure that's the whole story. Harvard, even then, gave scholarships to students as good as Ben.

It's possible that Ben's father needs Ben to help in the family soap and candle shop. That's what Ben does. Unfortunately, Ben hates his father's business. When the work isn't disgusting, it's dull. Ben makes the candles and soap by boiling large vats of animal fat and oil. For soap, the fat is mixed with lye, a chemical that can burn the skin and the lungs. The Franklin shop, like others of the time, sells goods that are practical rather than perfumed.

Soon after starting to work for his father, Ben begins to make comments about working on a ship instead. He's fascinated by the sailors and traders who pass through Boston. Fearing Ben will run away, his father decides to find him another trade.

Ben is placed with a relative who's a knife maker, but that arrangement lasts only a few days. The problem is that apprenticeships have to be bought. They're considered a kind of trade school, and the master tradesman demands a payment as if he were charging tuition. There's a signed contract, usually lasting seven

A colonial press

years. The apprentice isn't paid until the final year, if at all. He receives only meals and a place to live. (Apprenticeships for girls are rare.) An apprentice who wants to quit is out of luck. Breaking the contract can lead to a fine or even prison.

Unfortunately for Ben's father, the relative who owns the knife-making shop asks too much money for Ben's apprenticeship. James is the last choice.

Only twenty-one years old, James has just started

his business. He's counting on receiving a good fee to take on an apprentice. That won't happen if he takes Ben. Their father is expecting a favor for the family. This might explain why James demands that Ben's apprenticeship last nine years, an unusually long contract. Whatever the reason, from the start Ben feels it's not fair.

SILENCE IS GOLDEN

6:35 P.M.

The captain of his getaway ship still hasn't shown up. Ben is starting to wonder if James has learned of the plan. Then he sees his friend John Collins coming up the pier.

"I saw the captain taking his time at the pub, so I figured you'd be here," he says.

"Is everything still arranged?" Ben asks.

"Everything but the money. He'll expect that from you before you board."

Ben's work ranged from working the press to delivering the newspaper.

"I have it," Ben says. Earlier that day he sold his only possessions, his treasured books. It's enough for the voyage and a few days in New York. He expects to find work by then. "Are you sure he doesn't know my name?"

"He doesn't care. But if you make one up, stick to it until you get to New York."

If you make one up. Collins knows that's been Ben's specialty at the *Courant*, which prints articles written by James and his friends under pseudonyms like "Jack Dulman."

By coincidence, Ben's first alias, just like this one for the voyage to New York, was created to hide from James. Late one night, about a year and a half ago, he slipped an article for the *Courant* under the shop door. The author claimed to be an elderly widow living in the countryside outside Boston. Her name was Silence Dogood.

The next morning, everyone was charmed by the subtle insults the author aimed at the Massachusetts establishment. Although they knew the name was an alias, they didn't guess the person behind it was Ben. James wouldn't have published the article if he'd known. He was fooled like everyone else, so he jumped at it. He recognized that the author was poking fun at one of James's favorite targets, the clergyman Cotton Mather. Mather, widely considered the most educated man in the colonies, had played a big role in the Salem witch trials. The name "Silence Dogood" came from two of Mather's works: a sermon on "Holy Silence and Godly Patience" and

Cotton Mather

the book *Essays to Do Good*. Ben had created a character who was named after the Puritan virtues of Cotton Mather but who saw the world very differently.

Thirteen more of the Silence Dogood essays appeared in the next six months. Some expressed the serious ideas Ben was thinking about, like individual rights and community service. One attacked the governor of Massachusetts, calling him a "dangerous

hypocrite" who will "cheat a whole country."

Ben kept the secret of Silence's identity until the end. By the time James learned the truth, he had bigger problems than Ben's trick. The government had thrown him in jail because of the opinions printed in the

Courant. When he was released, he was ordered to let the government review the *Courant* before publication.

Refusing to accept censorship, James came up with a scheme to get around the order. Unfortunately for him, Ben saw an advantage for himself in it.

MY BROTHER'S KEEPER

7:35 P.M.

"Full moon," the captain says as he claps Ben around the shoulder. "Plenty of light to be on our way." The captain stinks of bad whiskey and stale tobacco.

Before they step onto the ship, Ben holds out his money. The captain takes it but doesn't look at it. He just stares Ben in the eye. After a moment he puts the money in his pocket and pushes Ben up the plank to the ship's deck. Ben knows he's passed a test, that he's been found trustworthy. He doesn't feel trustworthy. He's come this far by tricking his brother.

James got around the government by taking his

name off the newspaper. He signed legal documents to put the paper in Ben's hands. The issue of February 11, 1723, stated that the paper was "printed and sold by Benjamin Franklin."

To make the handover appear legal, James signed a document to end Ben's apprenticeship. In James's mind, this was just a way to fool the government. To protect himself, he made Ben sign a secret document confirming the apprenticeship.

> **"IT WAS NOT FAIR OF ME TO TAKE THIS ADVANTAGE [OF JAMES]. PERHAPS I WAS TOO SAUCY AND PROVOKING."**
>
> FROM *The Autobiography of Benjamin Franklin*

Ben knew he now had power over James. If James tried to prove that Ben was still an apprentice, James would have to admit that Ben didn't really take over the *Courant*. James would face a trial and probably go to jail.

Even so, Ben wasn't free yet. To keep Ben in line, James asked the other printers in town to refuse Ben a job.

So now Ben is running away. The tide is going out, the captain is shouting orders, and the boat is leaving the pier. Ben is standing out of the way of the deck-hands, watching as the church steeples of Boston get smaller and smaller. In days he'll be in New York, and not long after that he'll be in Philadelphia.

In time, he'll begin to regret the way he left James. A few years later he'll try to make things right between them. But he'll never regret the decision he is making tonight to leave Boston and begin his first great adventure. ❶

ONE **TWO** THREE FOUR FIVE SIX

DAY 2

TWO

DECEMBER 24,

1724

STRANDED

I t's about a year since he left Boston, and Ben hasn't rested for a moment. Staying in New York just a few days because there were no jobs for a printer, he quickly traveled to Philadelphia, the largest city in the colonies. There his skill and hard work caught the eye of Sir William Keith, Pennsylvania's governor. Keith declared Ben should have his own printing shop, and offered to be Ben's sponsor. Now he has sent Ben to London to buy equipment for the shop and to make business contacts. Ben is back on his feet—though after weeks of bad weather at sea, he's having a little trouble walking on land.

Gobbling a sweet roll from a cart near the docks, he takes in the commotion of the crowded, busy city. He's never seen so many people. And the buildings! The warehouses along the river Thames are taller than almost every building in America.

While he savors the first fresh food he's had since leaving Philadelphia, he keeps one hand tight against a coat pocket. He's carrying a small bundle of letters from the governor: letters of introduction to printers and a letter he can present to a bank for money.

He has memorized the first address, the shop of a private printer. London is a narrow maze of alleys and dead ends,

WHEN FRANKLIN ARRIVED IN LONDON, THE POPULATION WAS ABOUT 600,000—MORE THAN 300 TIMES THE SIZE OF PHILADELPHIA. ALL OF THE AMERICAN COLONIES HAD A POPULATION OF ONLY 450,000 EUROPEAN SETTLERS.

London in 1720

crowded with people rushing around with last-minute preparations for Christmas tomorrow. He has to ask for directions several times but eventually he finds the right street. There are several printers there. As he passes each one his excitement grows.

When he reaches the shop, he gives the letter to the owner. "This is from Sir William Keith, governor of Pennsylvania."

"Who?" the printer asks. "Never heard of him."

Ben's legs get weak again.

The printer opens the letter. "This isn't from any governor. The man who sent this is a scoundrel." He hands the letter back and coldly walks away from Ben.

What? Ben looks at the letter. He recognizes the name of the man who sent it, a crooked businessman

who passed through Philadelphia before Ben's ship left. He quickly checks the other letters. All of them are from the same man. He gets a sick feeling in his gut. These letters are less than worthless. They make him look like a friend of the crook. *Were*

Sir William Keith

there any others in the bag? he wonders.

He quickly leaves the shop and tries to find his way back to the docks. In his haste he keeps making wrong turns. As he loses time, the shops begin to close. Everyone is going home for Christmas Eve. He has to find the captain of his ship soon. He's furious with the governor. *Why would he do this to me?*

BEST LAID PLANS

While Ben's rushing through London, he's thinking back to Philadelphia and what led him here. A few months earlier, the governor seemed like a miracle. *Did I miss some warning?* He anxiously goes over it in his mind:

Within days of running away from Boston, he's working at the print shop in Philadelphia. His new boss is a bad printer, which makes Ben's skill shine more brightly. One day the governor comes into the shop, delighting Franklin's boss, who wants government business. Then the governor says he's there to see Ben. Ben's boss looks like he's been poisoned.

At a tavern down the street, the governor says the colony needs a printer like Ben. The governor will help Ben open a shop and will give Ben the work that Ben's boss wants. Ben is astonished and grateful. He heads back to Boston with a letter from the governor to Ben's father. If Ben's father will give Ben money to start the shop, the governor will make it successful.

By then, Ben has been away from Boston for seven months. He's had no contact with his family at all. They don't even know he is in Philadelphia. His return surprises them, as does his fancy new suit, his expensive watch, and his pocket full of money. Almost everyone is delighted to see him. Even Cotton Mather, who suffered Ben's attacks in James's newspaper, invites Ben to his home. But one person still won't forgive him. When Ben walks into James's shop, James looks at him sourly and turns back to work. Later, when Ben makes a point of embarrassing James by spreading money around to friends and family, James becomes even more angry.

Although Ben's father is pleased by the governor's letter, he isn't convinced Ben is ready for his own shop. He'd rather Ben and James end their feud and work together again. But James won't consider it, so their father gives Ben permission to return to Philadelphia. However, he doesn't give Ben money for a shop. Instead he gives Ben advice and a promise. He tells Ben to work hard and save money. If Ben doesn't have enough to open a shop by the time he turns twenty-one, his father will provide the rest.

The governor is surprised his offer was refused. "Since he won't set you up," the governor says, "I'll do it myself. Give me a list of what you need from England. You'll repay me when you can. We need a good printer here, and I'm sure you'll succeed."

Ben is overwhelmed. He thinks the governor is "one of the best men in the world." Later the governor says Ben should go to London himself. "Book your passage. I'll take care of the rest."

Only one ship a year travels from Philadelphia to London. It will leave in a couple of months. Ben makes his plans, then waits for the letters from the governor. Weeks go by. Each time Ben asks, the governor promises them for a later date. When Ben finally leaves Philadelphia, he's still empty-handed—and scared.

Fortunately the governor keeps his final promise: At the ship's last landing in America before the long voyage to Britain, Ben sees a sack of mail brought on board. It's closed with the official government seal. He breathes a relieved sigh.

The rough crossing is made easier by good company. Ben makes several friends, including the captain. A day before reaching London, the captain opens the mail sack so Ben can get an early start when the ship

lands. There are dozens of letters from the governor to various people in London. None are addressed to Ben. Though a few other letters in the sack are addressed to printers, they don't have the governor's seal. Ben figures they must be the ones for him anyway. He takes them.

But now the disaster with the printer tells him he's wrong. He's hoping the captain has the right letters on the ship—if he can even find the captain.

en keeps getting lost on the way back to the docks. The early winter darkness of London starts to fall. Ben tries the taverns and boardinghouses nearest the ship, but no one has seen the captain. Then he spots a friend from the ship. Ben explains what happened with the printer. The friend, who knows the governor, shakes his head.

"There's not any chance that he wrote any letters for you. He promises too much when he's excited, and then he can't face up to disappointing anyone."

"And the money?" Franklin asks.

"Impossible. He has no money himself. Didn't anyone tell you this in Philadelphia?"

"I didn't talk to anyone about the trip. I was afraid they'd try to take away the business before I returned. Now I can't return at all. I needed the money from the governor for my return voyage."

"Well, you're here now. There's no good reason to

go back immediately. The work you would do there, you can do here. And the printers here are the best in the world. You'll become more skilled than if you go back to Philadelphia."

"Without an introduction, how will I get a job?"

"You'll ask for one. If someone has a job, he'll give you a chance to prove your experience. How much money do you have? How long will it last here?"

"A week, maybe."

"If you haven't found work by then, come see me and I'll help you out."

Franklin heads back to the street of printers. There he sees a shop owned by a man named Samuel Palmer. He knows the name from books he's read. He remembers the high quality of the printing, and he likes the look of the large press he sees through the window. He gets up his courage and steps into the shop.

Thirty minutes later his sleeves are rolled up and he's throwing his weight behind the large handle of the press while his new boss smiles. **2**

POOR RICHARD

Philadelphia.

Franklin's hands are dirty with ink from printing today's edition of his newspaper, the *Pennsylvania Gazette*. There are smudges on his forehead and the sides of his face. The oily, still-wet ink on his leather apron is black and glistening.

Now twenty-six, after several years of honing his craft in London he's back in Philadelphia and has a thriving printing business of his own, courtesy of a friend.

While his assistants fold and bundle the last copies of the paper, Franklin selects a misprinted copy he set aside earlier, holding it by a corner to avoid making it messier. He spreads it on a worktable and, holding a brass ruler tightly against it, he carefully tears out an advertisement printed on the front page. Like a proud parent rereading a birth announcement, he's happy each time he reads it. He's given birth to another literary character, one he calls Richard Saunders— "Poor Richard."

The advertisement announces that Poor Richard has written an almanac—a calendar packed with all kinds of extra information about the weather and the seasons. In this time before electric lights and satellite weather radar, almanacs are useful references. Farmers use almanacs to decide when best to plant and pick crops. Sailors and fishermen use them to know high tides and low tides. To make an almanac attractive, printers add all the bonus features they can imagine. Some almanacs offer medical advice and recipes.

Until a couple of months ago, Franklin expected to print two almanacs written by other people. When both switched printers to save money, Franklin put pen to paper. He created his own almanac, better than the rest. *Poor Richard's Almanack* offers the usual information and more. The advertisement reads:

JUST PUBLISHED, FOR 1733, *Poor Richard: An Almanack*, CONTAINING THE LUNATIONS, ECLIPSES, PLANETS' MOTIONS AND ASPECTS, WEATHER, SUN AND MOON'S RISING AND SETTING, HIGH WATER, &C.; BESIDES MANY PLEASANT AND WITTY VERSES, JESTS, AND SAYINGS . . . BY RICHARD SAUNDERS. . . . PRINTED AND SOLD BY B. FRANKLIN.

Always eager to entertain, and sometimes desperate for filler, Franklin has loaded his almanac with bits of plainspoken philosophy: *He that lies down with dogs shall rise up with fleas. Great talkers, little doers. Fools make feasts and wise men eat 'em. Innocence is its own defense.*

Poor Richard, 1733.

AN

Almanack

For the Year of Chrift

1733,

Being the Firft after LEAP YEAR:

And makes fince the Creation	Years
By the Account of the Eaftern *Greeks*	7241
By the Latin Church, when ☉ ent. ♈	6932
By the Computation of *W.W.*	5742
By the *Roman* Chronology	5682
By the *Jewifh* Rabbies	5494

Wherein is contained

The Lunations, Eclipfes, Judgment of the Weather, Spring Tides, Planets Motions & mutual Afpects, Sun and Moon's Rifing and Setting, Length of Days, Time of High Water, Fairs, Courts, and obfervable Days.

Fitted to the Latitude of Forty Degrees, and a Meridian of Five Hours Weft from *London*, but may without fenfible Error, ferve all the adjacent Places, even from *Newfoundland* to *South-Carolina*.

By RICHARD SAUNDERS, Philom.

The cover of the first edition of Poor Richard's Almanack

He's also added a little controversy, a trick he learned back in his newspaper days with brother James. To amuse his readers, he's starting a public feud by making an eerie prediction. In the almanac, Poor Richard announces that long ago he used astrology to calculate the exact date and time when Mr. Titan Leeds, author of a competing almanac, will die. Mr. Leeds's time is almost up, says Poor Richard. He'll expire at 3:29 P.M. on October 17, 1733.

Leeds won't be amused, but readers will be.

REBOUND

ith good reason, Franklin is proud to have created his almanac quickly. The two almanac writers who took their business to another printer made a big mistake. There's no match for Franklin in any of the colonies as a writer or printer of something like this. His

advantage comes from his adventures during the nine years since he ran away from Boston.

After Titan Leeds really died five years later, Franklin dreamt up a note from Leeds's ghost conceding Richard's accuracy: "I did actually die at precisely the hour you mentioned, with a variation only of 5 minutes, 53 seconds." The ghost then predicted the death of another competitor!

After being fooled into sailing to London, where he arrived penniless, he quickly turned his fortunes around. He worked hard at Palmer's print shop and his reputation spread. The London printers admired his passion for the trade and his skill for it. He had a good mind for machinery, and printing is a trade with interesting machines. He also read a lot and wrote well, which helped when a customer asked what to say in an advertisement or on a poster.

For some jobs, Palmer let him do everything from start to finish. To set the type, Ben plucked metal letters one by one from large trays, arranging them to read backward so that the paper pressed against them will read in the correct direction. When he was done, he "beat" the ink onto it with two wood-handled leather balls. Then he laid a sheet of paper on top of it and slid it under the large plate of the press. He cranked the press's long handle to push the paper into the metal type with hundreds of pounds of force. Finally he slid out the tray, peeled off the paper, and hung it across a wire to dry.

He was also known for his colonial American habits. His colleagues, like most men in Britain, drank beer all through the day, starting in the morning. Drinking beer often took the place of a real meal. Franklin didn't drink alcohol, and he soon became known as the Water American. Some of his colleagues were annoyed by this. When he refused to contribute to a small communal drinking fund, they sabotaged his work. They mixed up the letters in his type and moved pages around on him right before he was ready to print. When he complained, they said the shop was haunted by a ghost! After three weeks of this, he gave in. He paid into the fund and he was welcomed back into the group, lesson learned. His lesson, that is. They hadn't learned theirs, which was that Franklin didn't give up easily. Instead of challenging them directly, he led by example until his influence was great enough to convince some of his coworkers to follow his habits. They began to start the day with porridge instead of beer, as Franklin did.

In his spare time, while his colleagues were at a tavern, he read. London was heaven to him because it was full of books. No shop in the colonies was as well stocked as an ordinary London bookshop. He also had access to dozens of newspapers and magazines that would never make it to the colonies.

A year and a half after arriving in London, now a successful young man with a good reputation and some money saved, he got an offer from the old friend from America who had given him advice the day he'd discovered Governor Keith had left him stranded. The friend was returning to America to open a shop in Philadelphia. He wanted Franklin to help him run it. He would pay Franklin's passage back to America and give him a good salary. It would be a little less money than Franklin was making, but Franklin would keep more of what he earned because Philadelphia was less expensive than London.

Franklin agreed. He knew his career in London was limited because he was an American. In Britain, only people born into the highest social class could truly succeed. The class system simply didn't allow people to make their own destiny, which Franklin was determined to do.

BORROWERS AND LENDERS

n Philadelphia, Franklin and his friend set up shop as planned. As well as working together, they stay in the same boardinghouse and eat meals together. His friend becomes like a father to him. Franklin respects him and loves him. Then tragedy: His friend becomes ill and dies.

Franklin has to go work for his old boss, the printer for whom he was working when he first met Governor Keith. It's an unhappy arrangement. They don't really like or trust each other. Franklin decides he has no choice but to open his own shop. Fortunately, people have noticed how hard he works and some are prepared to help him. Soon enough, he not only has a thriving business, but he owns the newspaper once published by his old boss, the *Pennsylvania Gazette*.

Franklin quickly outshines Philadelphia's other printers. It's not really a fair fight. Even the best of them is dull. He's also a voice of the government. Franklin likes to entertain his readers. Along with writing serious stories, he writes about subjects that newspapers still use to attract readers almost three hundred years later. He knows that crime stories sell newspapers—the more gruesome the story, the better. He creates an advice column, often writing the questions as well as the answers to make sure the column is interesting. He pokes fun at the powerful people the other newspaper defends.

Franklin's wit is what makes his newspaper such fun to read. Some of it comes from Franklin; a lot of it is borrowed from his extensive reading. That's one of the secrets behind *Poor Richard's Almanack.*

The name "Richard Saunders" is borrowed from a real-life astrologer and palm reader who lived in England in the 1600s and published an almanac of his own. Franklin borrowed the title *Poor Richard's* from his brother James, who has

> FRANKLIN'S ALMANAC INCLUDED PRACTICAL KNOWLEDGE SUCH AS THE DISTANCES BETWEEN CITIES, AND DIVERSIONS LIKE "A CATALOGUE OF THE PRINCIPAL KINGS AND PRINCES IN EUROPE." POOR RICHARD HIMSELF IS ON THE LIST: "POOR RICHARD, AN AMERICAN PRINCE, WITHOUT SUBJECTS, HIS WIFE BEING VICEROY OVER HIM."

been publishing an almanac in Rhode Island called *Poor Robin's*. The feud with Titan Leeds is a trick Franklin borrowed from the Irish writer Jonathan Swift, who had played the same game a couple of decades earlier in Britain. In the first issue of Swift's almanac, he predicted the death of a competitor whose almanac was filled with silly predictions. Even the little bits of common sense philosophy, which sound so American, come from Franklin's extensive reading of foreign books. He has a good eye for colorful details, and a gift for expressing them simply—often better than the original writer:

> "NOT A TENTH PART OF THE WISDOM WAS MY OWN."
>
> FROM *The Autobiography of Benjamin Franklin*

- *An ounce of prevention is worth a pound of cure.*
- *Early to bed and early to rise makes a man healthy, wealthy and wise.*
- *Three may keep a secret, if two of them are dead.*

- *Fish and visitors stink in three days.*

- *God helps them that help themselves.*

- *Wink at small faults; remember you have great ones.*

- *Haste makes waste.*

- *No gains without pains.*

- *Half the truth is often a great lie.*

POOR RICHARD, RICH BEN

well-dressed woman enters the shop and waits impatiently as Franklin wipes his hands clean and approaches the counter. The woman produces a sheet of paper containing the details of her daughter's coming marriage. She'd like an announcement printed.

"Of course, madam," Franklin says. Then he casually adds, "I see the marriage is three months hence. Have you checked to see whether there will be enough moonlight that evening for guests to travel home safely?" A minute later he's made his first sale.

This first edition will sell so quickly that Franklin will have to reprint it two times in the next month. Booksellers all over the colonies will take copies for their customers.

Franklin will keep the almanac going for twenty-five years. Just about the time he stops publishing it, he'll collect the proverbs about money into a single book. *The Way to Wealth* will become one of the most popular books in history. Franklin will certainly enjoy having the regular income from the almanac—*Nothing but money is sweeter than honey*, Poor Richard tells his readers—but more important for history, his wealth will free his time for his later scientific experiments and his work for the colonies.

As the customer with the first copy leaves the shop, Franklin allows himself a moment of pride. He knows he's earned it. Or, as Poor Richard will later put it, *A life of leisure and a life of laziness are two different things. No man ever was glorious who was not laborious.* ③

*A cartoon makes fun of Franklin's practice of
distilling the wisdom of other writers into books of his own.*

LIGHTNING IN
A BOTTLE

Philadelphia. 7:45 A.M.

ranklin looks out his window and is frustrated by what he sees. Today is exactly one year since carpenters started to build the new steeple of Christ Church, just down the street from his house. They aren't close to being done.

Franklin wants that steeple. His desire has nothing to do with the church itself, which has been one of Philadelphia's largest buildings for more than twenty years. He wants it because he's been waiting to try a new scientific experiment. Already retired from daily printing work at the young age of forty-six, he's been dabbling in the new field of electricity. Today, to test his belief that lightning is electricity, he wants to draw lightning from the sky. But without the steeple, he can't reach high enough.

It turns out, however, that his reach is greater than he knows. Almost four thousand miles away, in a town just north of Paris, France, a retired soldier is following Franklin's instructions for the experiment that Franklin hasn't yet had a chance to try himself.

ALL THE KING'S MEN

bout ten years earlier, Franklin had been fascinated by a traveling entertainer who performed tricks with static electricity. It looked like magic, but Franklin knew it was science.

He had to understand it. At the time, people knew a little about what electricity did, but they didn't understand why it happened. Franklin began to experiment with it himself.

After making several interesting discoveries, he described his work in letters to a friend in London. He hoped the letters would be published by the Royal Society, a group of Britain's best scientists. The Society, however, wasn't interested in the work of a colonial amateur. This turned out to be for the best. A privately published book of the letters was read widely, and soon it was translated into French and German.

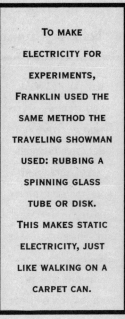

TO MAKE ELECTRICITY FOR EXPERIMENTS, FRANKLIN USED THE SAME METHOD THE TRAVELING SHOWMAN USED: RUBBING A SPINNING GLASS TUBE OR DISK. THIS MAKES STATIC ELECTRICITY, JUST LIKE WALKING ON A CARPET CAN.

Franklin's letters explain essential facts about electricity that are still taught today. We even use the words Franklin chose. He was the first scientist to say electricity has "charges" that are "positive" or "negative," which he shortened to "plus" and "minus." After making a device to store an electrical charge, he called it a "battery."

In France, one of the first readers of Franklin's book was a man who knew King Louis XV. Georges-Louis Leclerc de Buffon was in charge of the royal botanical garden, which he used for scientific research. Fascinated by Franklin's experiments, he duplicated them and helped to publicize Franklin's work.

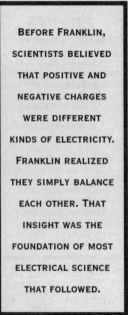

BEFORE FRANKLIN, SCIENTISTS BELIEVED THAT POSITIVE AND NEGATIVE CHARGES WERE DIFFERENT KINDS OF ELECTRICITY. FRANKLIN REALIZED THEY SIMPLY BALANCE EACH OTHER. THAT INSIGHT WAS THE FOUNDATION OF MOST ELECTRICAL SCIENCE THAT FOLLOWED.

Soon after, the king of France asked for a demonstration. He was thrilled by what he saw. His amazement made Buffon and other French scientists even more eager to study Franklin's theories.

The first thing they wanted to try was Franklin's

plan for a lightning experiment. Franklin devised it after noticing that electrical charges and lightning had many similarities. He had made a list in his notebook:

1. Giving light. 2. Color of the light. 3. Crooked direction. 4. Swift motion. 5. Being conducted by metals. 6. Crack or noise in exploding. 7. Subsisting [continuing to exist] in water or ice. 8. Rending [splitting] bodies it passes through. 9. Destroying animals. 10. Melting metals. 11. Firing inflammable substances. 12. Sulfurous smell. . . . We do not know whether this property is in lightning. But since they agree [are similar] in all the particulars wherein we can already compare them, is it not probable they agree likewise in this? Let the experiment be made.

This is the plan that appears in his book:

To determine the question, whether the clouds

that contain lightning are electrified or not, I would propose an experiment to be try'd where it may be done conveniently. On the top of some high tower or steeple, place a kind of a sentry box [a small shed] big enough to contain a man and an electrical stand. From the middle of the stand let an iron rod rise, and pass bending out of the door, and then upright 20 or 30 feet, pointed very sharp at the end. If the electrical stand be kept clean and dry, a man standing on it when such clouds are passing low, might be electrified, and afford sparks, the rod drawing fire to him from the cloud.

Franklin doesn't know that on this very morning, while he's in Philadelphia grumbling about the lack of progress at the church, a volunteer in France, where it's already afternoon, waits near a sentry box built with an iron rod extending forty feet into the air.

In the town of Marly-la-Ville, low, dark clouds are threatening. There's a lightning strike in the distance, followed by loud thunder. The volunteer rushes inside the sentry box with a small glass jar that has a brass wire sticking out of the top. As the clouds pass overhead, he brings the wire near the iron rod. When the wire is close to the rod, but not quite touching, a spark flies from the rod to the wire with a "crackling noise." Electricity! He tries it again, and gets a stronger spark.

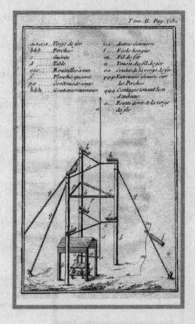

The sentry box built at Marly-la-Ville.
The tall iron rod is supported by wood.

Hail is falling now. Some townspeople who have been watching nervously now back away from the sentry box, convinced there will be an explosion. A child runs to fetch the local clergyman. From the garbled explanation, the clergyman thinks the volunteer has been killed. He runs through the hail to the sentry box and finds the volunteer playing with the sparks. The volunteer lets him try. For fifteen minutes, while the brief storm lasts, they draw sparks from the rod. The clergyman then rushes home to write down his observations.

> THE EXPERIMENT AS DESIGNED BY FRANKLIN IS VERY DANGEROUS. A RUSSIAN SCIENTIST WAS KILLED ATTEMPTING IT. THE CLERGYMAN AT MARLY-LA-VILLE RECEIVED A STRONG SHOCK TO HIS ARM. DO NOT TRY IT!

By the end of the day, Buffon will report to the king of France that the extraordinary American has shown humankind how to capture lightning from the heavens. Franklin is about to become the most famous man in the world.

The link Franklin has made between lightning and electricity has an immediate practical use. Using Franklin's design, lightning rods will soon be attached to buildings all over Europe, reducing fires and deaths by guiding the electrical charge safely into the ground.

John Adams, who will later become America's second president, is no friend of Franklin, yet even he will admit Franklin becomes beloved because of this discovery. As Adams says, it "almost annihilated that panic, terror and superstitious horror which was once almost universal in violent storms of thunder and lightning." Adams adds:

> *Nothing, perhaps, that ever occurred upon this earth was so well calculated to give any man an extensive and universal celebrity as the discovery of the efficacy of iron points and the invention*

of lightning rods. The idea was one of the most sublime that ever entered a human imagination, that a mortal should disarm the clouds of heaven, and almost "snatch from His hand the sceptre and the rod!" . . . Franklin's fame was universal. His name was familiar to government and people, to kings, courtiers, nobility, clergy, and philosophers. . . . There was scarcely a peasant or a citizen, a valet de chambre, coachman or footman, a lady's chambermaid or a scullion in a kitchen, who was not familiar with it, and who did not consider him as a friend to human kind. When they spoke of him, they seemed to think he was to restore the golden age.

In time, this reputation will become important to America. About twenty-five years from this day, Franklin will win France's help against Britain. His celebrity will help make the difference between victory and defeat in the Revolutionary War.

Today, however, Franklin is just a frustrated scientist. He's tired of waiting for the church steeple to be raised.

A few streets in the opposite direction is an empty field with an abandoned shed. Almost every day he walks by it and imagines it could serve as a perfect sentry box for his experiment if only it were higher.

In another month, when the letter with the good news from Paris is still on a ship crossing the Atlantic, Franklin will walk by the field one more time and get an idea: a kite! Then he'll try his experiment himself and discover he's right. ➍

> BEFORE FRANKLIN, LIGHTNING WAS THOUGHT TO COME FROM A DEMON OR TO BE A SIGN OF GOD'S ANGER. IN MANY COUNTRIES, PEOPLE BELIEVED THEY COULD PROTECT THEMSELVES BY RINGING CHURCH BELLS. THEY COULDN'T HAVE BEEN MORE WRONG. THE COMBINATION OF HIGH CHURCH STEEPLES AND LARGE METAL BELLS ATTRACTED LIGHTNING. A LOT OF BELL RINGERS DIED.

DAY FIVE

JANUARY 15, 1758

A DANGEROUS MAN

London. 9:45 A.M.

All morning long Franklin has been having a bad feeling about today. He's going to meet with Thomas Penn, the son of Pennsylvania's founder, William Penn. Thomas doesn't merely govern the colony. He owns it. Legally, Pennsylvania is a business. Several decades earlier, King Charles II of England owed Thomas's father a lot of money. As payment, William accepted land in America that could be sold to colonists.

After William died, Thomas inherited the colony. He still owns most of the land. Much of what he no longer owns he controls through private contracts.

He has more power over the lives of the colonists than a governor appointed by a monarch would have.

Thomas Penn

Today Franklin will be fighting him about just how much power that is. The Pennsylvania Assembly, which represents the citizens of the colony, has voted for a property tax that Penn doesn't want to pay. The question is, do the Assembly's laws apply to everyone, or is the Penn family above the laws written by the people?

This dispute is the reason the Assembly asked Franklin, now fifty-two years old and one of the colony's most respected citizens, to go to London.

Franklin is supposed to find a compromise. Unfortunately, after six months he has made no progress. Penn doesn't even want to meet with him. Instead, Penn has been using newspaper advertisements and government connections to prevent Franklin from winning support in Parliament. Franklin has also been using the press and working behind the scenes.

What's happening between Franklin and Penn is more than a political disagreement. By the end of today, Franklin will have made the greatest enemy of his life.

FATHER KNOWS BEST

As Franklin dresses for the meeting—in his six months in London he has found a good tailor—he goes over what he plans to say: All the Pennsylvanians want are the rights that Thomas's father, William Penn, granted to them decades earlier. It's a simple argument, which Franklin knows is best when facing a complicated dispute, and it seems to be supported by Pennsylvania's legal history. Still, Franklin is uneasy. He knows Thomas Penn is nothing like William Penn was.

Franklin, like nearly every other Pennsylvanian, admires the memory of William Penn. His generosity was famous. Although the charter he received from King Charles II of England to establish Pennsylvania had made him the "true and absolute" owner of the colony, William Penn immediately created what he called a Frame of Government to share power with citizens and guarantee their rights. He was true to his Quaker belief in pacifism and made honorable treaties with Native Americans, who had good feelings toward him long afterward. He believed Pennsylvania should be open to all religions, not just to Quakers.

Thomas's reputation is not as honorable. He's known as a slippery businessman who doesn't keep his word. Many years earlier he lost the goodwill of the Native Americans by tricking them out of land. More recently he tried to block peace treaties with Native Americans who were allied with France. He tried to prevent Roman Catholics from worshipping and, in some cases, even from settling in Pennsylvania. He's especially tough with Quakers, because their religious beliefs frustrate his effort to govern as he likes. Shortly before Franklin was sent to London, Penn tried a legal maneuver to force Quakers out of the Pennsylvania Assembly. He wanted Parliament to require that all members of the Assembly take an oath of loyalty. The religious beliefs of Quakers prevent them from taking any such oaths. His scheme almost worked.

WILLIAM PENN AGREED TO IMPROVEMENTS IN THE FRAME OF GOVERNMENT REQUESTED BY THE COLONISTS. THE LIBERTY BELL WAS CREATED TO MARK THE FIFTIETH ANNIVERSARY OF THE FOURTH AND FINAL VERSION, ALSO KNOWN AS THE CHARTER OF PRIVILEGES. IT GUARANTEED RELIGIOUS FREEDOM AND OTHER RIGHTS.

It's possible that he's cold and selfish because of what happened to his generous father. William Penn expected to regain the money the king owed him, and more, by selling land to settlers. Yet William died penniless, and his family was left with large debts. An adviser had stolen his money years earlier.

Thomas has restored the family's finances. He lives in England and treats Pennsylvania simply as a source of money, not as the sanctuary of religious and political freedom that his father imagined.

He's a tough adversary for the Pennsylvanians. His political connections are strong, and he uses them cleverly. One of his closest associates is Lord Carteret, Lord President of the Privy Council, which gives advice to King George III. Franklin once thought Carteret might be helpful in the dispute with Penn. But a few days ago he had a meeting with Carteret that he now fears is a sign of what will happen today. What Carteret said was so alarming that Franklin immediately sent a report to the Pennsylvania Assembly:

He received me with great civility; and after some questions respecting the state of affairs in America he said to me:

"You Americans have wrong ideas of the nature of your constitution; you contend that the king's instructions to his governors are not laws, and think yourselves at liberty to regard or disregard them at your own discretion. But these instructions are not like the pocket instructions given to a minister going abroad, for regulating his conduct in some trifling point of ceremony. They are drawn up by judges learned in the laws; they are then considered, debated and perhaps amended in council, after which they are signed by the king.

"They are then, so far as they relate to you, the law of the land for the king is the legislator of the colonies."

I told his Lordship that this was new doctrine to me. I had always understood from our charters

that our laws were to be made by our assemblies,
to be presented indeed to the king for his royal
assent, but that being once given the king could
not repeal or alter them.

Franklin is worried that the British government has already decided that American laws are not to be made by Americans, and that Americans do not and should not enjoy the same rights as British citizens. The Revolutionary War will be fought because of stubborn opinions like these.

LIKE FATHER, LIKE SON?

ranklin's anger makes him tense even before he arrives at Penn's residence. As he's ushered into Penn's luxurious office, he can tell from Penn's face that Penn is angry too.

Penn has been wary of Franklin for a long time.

About ten years ago, Franklin acted independently of Penn to create a militia for the colony's defense. Penn said that Franklin's actions were almost "treason." He called Franklin "a dangerous man," adding, "I should be very glad he inhabited any other country."

Penn knows he has an advantage this time. Franklin isn't surrounded by American supporters. "Mr. Franklin's popularity is nothing here," Penn told a friend. "He will be looked very coldly upon by great people."

William Penn

Neither man can keep his cool for long, and very quickly the conversation becomes undiplomatic. Franklin is blunt: William Penn's charter gives the Pennsylvania Assembly "all the powers and privileges of an assembly according to the rights of freeborn subjects of England," he says. It's all

Franklin in about 1748

right there in the original charter, backed up by fifty years of
Pennsylvania history.

Franklin has underestimated
his opponent. Penn agrees with
Franklin that the charter offers
those rights. "But," he adds, "my
father granted privileges he was
not by a Royal charter empow-
ered to grant."

TWENTY YEARS
BEFORE THIS MEETING,
THOMAS PENN HAD
BOUGHT SOMETHING
AT FRANKLIN'S
PRINTING SHOP
BUT HADN'T PAID
THE BILL. FRANKLIN
NEVER FORGOT IT!

Franklin can't believe what
he is hearing. Penn's legal position is that his father,
William, was a swindler.

"Then if your father had no right to grant privileges he pretended to grant . . . those who came to
settle in the province on the faith of that grant . . .
were deceived, cheated and betrayed."

"They should have looked into that themselves,"
Penn replies. "The Royal charter was no secret. If anyone came into the province on my father's offer of

privileges, well, if they were deceived by that it was their own fault." Penn laughs as he says this.

At first Franklin is too angry to speak, but he knows his anger is obvious anyway. Finally, with disgust, he says, "The people who came on the promise of your father were not lawyers, and trusting your father they did not think to consult any."

Penn shrugs. He message is: *Sue me.*

Franklin realizes there's no point in saying more, and Penn is happy to end the conversation there.

Walking home to clear his head, Franklin devises a bold plan for revenge. He'll steal the whole colony from Penn.

His idea is to convince Parliament and the king to take over Pennsylvania as a royal colony, which will give Pennsylvanians more rights than they enjoy under Penn's ownership.

In his anger, he's making two great errors.

Penn is powerful and rich, giving him more influence with British politicians than Franklin enjoys.

Franklin has chosen an enemy he can't defeat. Within a few days, Penn will write to a colleague that Franklin is a "malicious villain . . . I will not have any conversation with him on any pretense." Franklin observes, "When I meet [Penn] anywhere, there appears on his countenance a strange mixture of hatred, anger, fear and fixation."

Franklin's other mistake is to trust that King George III is reasonable. He'll waste almost a decade trying win over the king. In that time, he'll behave like a loyal subject. Meanwhile, back in America the people will become intensely frustrated by British rule. They won't look closely enough to see the diplomatic game Franklin is playing. In the struggle between the colonies and Great Britain, Franklin is about to be accused of treason by both sides. **5**

"FORCE OF ARMS"

London. 1:25 P.M.

Q. What is your Name, and Place of abode?

A. Franklin, of Philadelphia . . .

Q. What was the temper of America towards Great Britain before the year 1763?

A. The best in the world. They submitted willingly to the government of the Crown, and paid, in all their courts, obedience to acts of parliament . . .

Q. And what is their temper now?

A. Oh, very much altered . . .

A mistake by Franklin today could threaten the lives of his family.

Americans are rioting in opposition to a new tax law, the Stamp Act. The law says a government stamp must be purchased for all sorts of items. Any contract requires a stamp. A ship can't be loaded or unloaded until the cargo list bears a stamp. A stamp is required to make a college degree official. Calendars and almanacs require a stamp. Newspapers require a stamp, as do individual advertisements within them. A stamp is even required for a deck of playing cards. The prices range from a few pennies to the equivalent of several hundred dollars in modern money.

This is certainly the most treacherous moment of Franklin's career. Franklin, like the British politicians, is far removed from the events in America. The long delays in communication—it takes weeks at best for mail to cross the Atlantic, but more commonly months—is one reason he's in this trouble. He had tried to prevent Parliament from passing the Stamp Act, but, once it was passed, he believed America would simply have to live with it. This was a serious misjudgment of the mood in America. His opinions became public because he was given the opportunity to choose the stamp commissioner for Pennsylvania. He nominated a friend. Back in America, his critics said this meant he wanted to profit from the tax. In Philadelphia, his wife has had to barricade herself with a pistol in an upstairs room of their house. A bullying mob was ready to tear the house down before a crowd of Franklin's supporters warned them to stay away.

Today in London he's the one facing an angry crowd. For the next several hours, Parliament will interrogate him. He knows that what he says and how he says it will be examined carefully by Americans who have come to believe he's a traitor.

Franklin, sixty years old, stands through this testimony, and he'll remain standing for almost four hours. James Hewitt, an ally, starts the questioning.

"Do the Americans pay any considerable taxes among themselves?"

"Certainly many, and very heavy taxes," Franklin answers.

"Are not the colonies very able to pay the stamp duty?"

"In my opinion, there is not gold and silver enough in the colonies to pay the stamp duty for one year."

Hewitt is giving Franklin a chance to make his case, which is supported by Britain's new prime minister, Lord Rockingham. But all of the questioning won't be easy.

The reports of marauding gangs of rebels in America are astonishing. In Boston, the crowd hanged a stuffed dummy representing a government official and then paraded it through the streets and set it on fire in front of the official's house. While it was burning,

they threw rocks at his house and through his windows. The next night they descended on the home of the governor of Massachusetts. They spent the night ransacking the house and tearing down chunks of its brick walls and its roof. Scenes like these are taking place all

Rioters in Boston

over the colonies. In some ports, the British can't even unload the stamps. A ship carrying stamps for New Jersey is left anchored far offshore. In South Carolina, a platoon of fourteen soldiers guards the stamps, but those soldiers are no match for a mob of one hundred and fifty angry colonists who take the stamps and burn them.

Americans are also refusing to buy British goods. British merchants are finding that their partners in America can't unload the ships carrying goods for which the British merchants have already paid. In England, an estimated fifty thousand men are out of work because of the halt in trade with America.

A newspaper prints its own obituary. Rather than submit to the act, the owner chose to stop publication. The text around the skull and bones in the corner reads, "An emblem of the effects of the stamp."

Patrick Henry, who ten years later will declare, "Give me liberty or give me death!" lists his objections in a furious speech to the Virginia House of Burgesses, the colonial assembly. He declares that the settlers of America have brought with them the rights they enjoyed in Britain; that the charters of the individual colonies confirm those rights; that those rights have always been asserted and recognized during the history of the colonies; and therefore the colonists enjoy the same rights as any British subject.

That means Americans, like Britons, can only be taxed by representatives they elect. "No taxation without representation" is the war cry.

"YOUR OPPRESSIONS!"

he interrogation of Franklin is no longer friendly. He's being asked about the French and Indian War, which recently ended and which is directly related to the Stamp Act.

The French and Indian War, which lasted from 1754 to 1763, was fought for control of America's western frontier. At the time, the frontier started just a few hundred miles from the shore of the Atlantic Ocean. The British colonists fought against French settlers and some Native American tribes.

The war was part of a larger conflict in Europe,

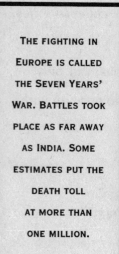

THE FIGHTING IN EUROPE IS CALLED THE SEVEN YEARS' WAR. BATTLES TOOK PLACE AS FAR AWAY AS INDIA. SOME ESTIMATES PUT THE DEATH TOLL AT MORE THAN ONE MILLION.

and now that the fighting is over, Britain is left with a large debt. The Stamp Act is meant to repay that debt and to pay for soldiers who will hold the territory gained in the war.

The colonists recognize the need to repay the debt, and they are willing to pay taxes to do it. They simply believe they have a right, just as British subjects living in Britain have a right, to determine what kind of taxes they will pay.

A hostile member of Parliament asks Franklin, "Do you think it right America should be protected by this country, and pay no part of the expense?"

"That is not the case," Franklin replies calmly. "The colonies raised, clothed and paid, during the last war, near twenty-five thousand men, and spent many millions." Franklin has all the statistics ready.

A couple of days earlier one member of Parliament expressed the government's view: "Will these Americans, children planted by our care, nourished up by our indulgence until they are grown to a degree of strength and opulence, and protected by our arms, will they grudge to contribute their might to relieve us from the heavy weight of that burden which we lie under?"

His argument was met by a member of Parliament who had fought alongside the colonists in the war: "Planted by your care? No! Your oppressions planted them in America. . . . Nourished by your indulgence? They grew by your neglect of them. . . . Protected by your arms? They have nobly taken up arms in your defense."

Former prime minister George Grenville, author of the Stamp Act, joined in the debate to complain about the Americans. "Protection and obedience are reciprocal. Great Britain protects America; America is bound to yield obedience. If not, tell me when the Americans were emancipated?"

William Pitt, a supporter of the colonists, answered him, "The gentleman asks, when were the colonies emancipated? I desire to know, when were they made slaves?"

STAND AND DELIVER

In the past four hours, Franklin has answered almost two hundred questions. About half of those were scripted with friends in Parliament to make sure the colonists' arguments were part of the interrogation. The other half came from members of Parliament who are hostile to the colonists. He hopes today's testimony will convince Americans that he understands their anger.

The final question is the most important: If Parliament repeals the Stamp Act, will the Americans stop asking for rights?

Franklin knows he's being offered a political compromise. Normally, he believes compromise is important in politics. He thinks that without it there's little chance of progress. But he also knows that he can't allow any compromise today.

They'll never give in, he says, "unless compelled by force of arms."

The testimony is over. Franklin is exhausted. Though the thick cloth of his coat conceals the fact, he has sweated through his underclothes. Worse than the physical strain has been the strain on his nerves. Although Franklin was slow to understand the depth of the colonists' anger, after he came around, he became a dynamo. His intense work over the last months, one eyewitness said, "is really astonishing."

Before he leaves, some of his supporters come over to shake his hand. His friend the prime minister is one.

"It's done," Lord Rockingham says. "The law will be struck within the week." Rockingham is almost right. It takes only slightly longer, but the Stamp Act is struck down.

Franklin is glad to hear his opinion, but he's still worried. Rockingham understands.

"Your countrymen will learn soon enough what you've done today," Rockingham says. He winks at Franklin. Parliamentary meetings like this one are supposed to be secret, but everyone knows that unofficial transcripts are published in the newspapers almost immediately. He's right about that, too. Franklin's testimony restores his reputation. More important, the mobs never threaten his family again. **6**

The EXAMINATION of Doctor BENJAMIN FRANKLIN, before an August Assembly, relating to the Repeal of the STAMP-ACT, &c.

Q. WHAT is your name, and place of abode?

A. Franklin, of Philadelphia.

Q. Do the Americans pay any confiderable taxes among themfelves?

A. Certainly many, and very heavy taxes.

Q. What are the prefent taxes in Pennfylvania, laid by the laws of the Colony?

A. There are taxes on all eftates real and perfonal, a poll tax, a tax on all offices, profeffions, trades and bufineffes, according to their profits; an excife on all wine, rum, and other fpirits; and a duty of Ten Pounds per head on all Negroes imported, with fome other duties.

Q. For what purpofes are thofe taxes laid?

A. For the fupport of the civil and military eftablifhments of the country, and to difcharge the heavy debt contracted in the laft war.

Q. How long are thofe taxes to continue?

A. Thofe for difcharging the debt are to continue till 1772, and longer, if the debt fhould not be then all difcharged. The others muft always continue.

Q. Was it not expected that the debt would have been fooner difcharged?

A. It was, when the peace was made with France and Spain——But a frefh war breaking out with the Indians, a frefh load of debt was incurred, and the taxes, of courfe, continued longer by a new law.

Q. Are not all the people very able to pay thofe taxes?

A. No. The frontier counties, all along the continent, having been frequently ravaged by the enemy, and greatly impoverifhed, are able to pay very little tax. And therefore, in confideration of their diftreffes, our late tax laws do exprefly favour thofe counties, excufing the fufferers; and I fuppofe the fame is done in other governments.

Q. Are not you concerned in the management of the Poft-Office in America?

A. Yes. I am Deputy Poft-Mafter General of North-America.

Q. Don't you think the diftribution of ftamps, by poft, to all the inhabitants, very practicable, if there was no oppofition?

A. The pofts only go along the fea coafts; they do not, except in a few inftances, go back into the country; and if they did, fending for ftamps by poft would occafion an expence of poftage, amounting, in many cafes, to much more than that of the ftamps themfelves.

Q. Are you acquainted with Newfoundland?

A. I never was there.

Q. Do you know whether there are any poft roads on that ifland?

A. I have heard that there are no roads at all; but that the communica-

An early transcript of Franklin's testimony

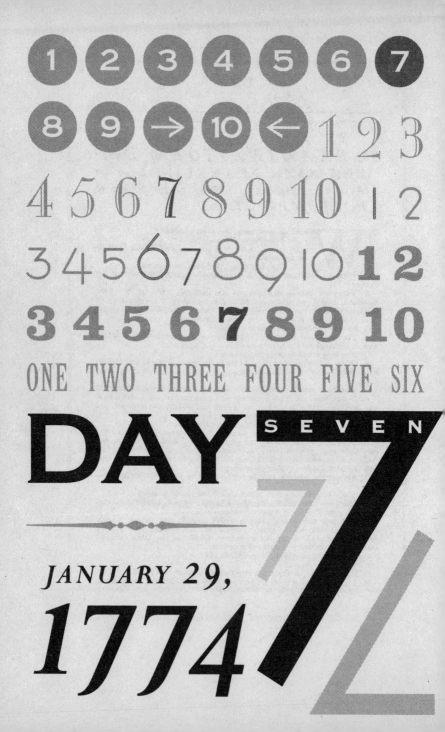

DAY SEVEN 7

ONE TWO THREE FOUR FIVE SIX

JANUARY 29, 1774

AMBUSHED

London.

awn in Hyde Park: Two Englishmen stand twenty paces apart, pointing identical pistols at each other. They fire. It takes a moment for them to realize their shots have missed.

"Satisfied?" one man shouts to the other.

"No."

"Then it's swords."

Swords are handed over by friends. The men begin to cut at each other furiously. The ringing of steel against steel echoes in the field. Just as the better swordsman is about to strike a finishing blow, he slips on the dewy grass. His opponent's sword pierces his shoulder and he collapses in pain.

The fight is to first blood, not to the death, so it's over; but neither man is satisfied. The argument that led to this stupid contest isn't settled. Each has accused the other of a serious theft, and the accusations still stand.

The stolen items are letters written by the royal governor of Massachusetts, Thomas Hutchinson. The letters have been published in a Boston newspaper, creating a scandal in London and sparking riots in America. Hutchinson wants "restraint of liberty." He wants troops sent from Britain to police the colonists. He thinks rebel leaders should probably be executed.

The colonists want to run Hutchinson out of office. They were already angry at him at the time of the Stamp Act a few years earlier, when the letters were written. A mob burned down his house then.

Now that the letters are public, the colonists are calling for his head. Rebellion has broken out again.

A CONFESSION

Today, six weeks after the duel, Franklin will become an unexpected victim of it. The moment he heard about it he worried there'd be trouble. He knows that neither man caused the scandal. He did.

A bundle of thirteen letters had been sent to him in London anonymously. He was the one who sent them to rebel leaders in Boston. He asked that the letters be kept private, but the Bostonians were too angry for that.

Franklin decides he must confess. He writes a newspaper statement that declares the two duelists are "totally ignorant and innocent of the whole affair." He adds, admirably but not entirely honestly, "I alone am the person who obtained and transmitted to Boston the letters in question."

This confession is more of a problem for Franklin than for an ordinary citizen. Along with his other duties, Franklin is deputy postmaster general for the colonies, a royal appointment. He appears to be abusing his government office.

Still, he doesn't back down. In his confession he announces that he was right to release the letters, saying they are public documents and meant "to incense the Mother Country against her Colonies."

The British goverment isn't happy. Franklin is summoned to a fierce interrogation about the affair.

THE COCKPIT

The most powerful men in England, the king's advisers known as the Privy Council, hold their meetings in a room originally used for royal rooster fighting. They call it "the Cockpit." Today it's Franklin who's under attack. Now sixty-eight years old, he's standing before three dozen council members, ready for a grilling. Many prominent men have crowded into the arena to watch. Breaking with tradition, women have come too.

So many people have come because news of an extraordinary event in the colonies has reached London. Protesting a new tax on tea, thousands of Bostonians mobbed the wharves of Boston Harbor, where three ships filled with tea were waiting to unload their cargo. A band of protesters boarded the ships, broke open 342 crates, and dumped the tea into the harbor.

The Privy Council is infuriated by this "Boston Tea Party." Franklin has tried to prepare himself for the worst, but today will be tougher than he ever imagined. The government's chief lawyer, Alexander Wedderburn, is considered "one of the nastiest, most unscrupulous, most ambitious politicians" in Britain.

THE BOSTONIANS PAYING THE EXCISE-MAN OR TARRING & FEATHERING

*A cartoon of Bostonians attacking a tax collector. In the
background, tea is being dumped over the side of a ship.*

The battle begins with a formality. Franklin reads aloud a petition asking for the removal of Governor Hutchinson. The Massachusetts Assembly is peacefully relying on the king's "wisdom and goodness."

Wedderburn ignores the petition. He lets loose an angry attack that lasts almost an hour:

"Nothing will acquit Dr. Franklin of obtaining [the letters] by fraudulent or corrupt means, for the most malignant of purposes. . . . I hope, my lords, you will mark and brand this man, for the honor of this country, of Europe, and of mankind. He has forfeited all the respect of societies and of men. Into what companies will he hereafter go with an unembarrassed face or the honest intrepidity of virtue? Men will watch him with a jealous eye; they will hide their papers from him and lock up their [writing desks]. . . ."

Wedderburn paces the length of the Cockpit, addressing each of the thirty-six members of the Privy Council, barely acknowledging Franklin's presence.

"My lords, Dr. Franklin's mind may have been so

possessed with the idea of a great American republic that he may easily slide into the language of the minister of foreign independent state. A foreign ambassador might bribe a villain to steal or betray any state papers; he is under the command of another state. . . . But Dr. Franklin is a subject [of Great Britain's], and if the subject injure a subject he is answerable to the law."

Through all of this, Franklin shows no emotion. He stands still, with no expression on his face.

He can hear behind him the quiet laughter and snide comments of the men and women who have come to watch. There's a murmur of agreement from them when the government's lawyer accuses Franklin of trying to remove Hutchinson so Franklin can become governor of Massachusetts.

Franklin declines to respond to the attack, and the Privy Council immediately votes to dismiss the petition. Hutchinson will stay in office.

As the meeting breaks up, several members of the Privy Council and some of the audience congratulate the government's lawyer. Franklin, exhausted, slips quietly out of the Cockpit and returns home.

Later that evening, a friend comes to visit. Franklin seems calm about what happened. It's just part of public life, he says. But behind the calm facade he's angry. What happened today has changed his attitude toward Great Britain forever. He's endured all the condescension he can take. He'll no longer work hard to preserve the relationship between America and Great Britain. He tells his visitor he's certain a decision has already been made that evening to remove him from his postmaster appointment. It's only a matter of time before he'll be forced to leave London. He's sad about that.

As he and his friend talk about his plans, eyewitnesses to the scene in the Cockpit are talking to journalists. Soon reports will appear in London papers and be sent back to America. Despite the momentary damage to his reputation in London, his reputation in America will soon be greater than ever before. Hearing the news of the battle with the Privy Council, a friend remarked, "As a result of this humiliation, Franklin is a very popular character in every part of America. He will be received and carried in triumph to his house when he arrives amongst us. . . . [He will be] handed down to posterity among the first and greatest characters in the world." **7**

"UNLUCKY EXPRESSIONS"

Philadelphia. 11:05 A.M.

ranklin is watching some of the best minds in America argue over small phrases and obscure definitions. Future generations will call these men the Founding Fathers, but right now Franklin thinks they're acting like young children. Having seen this kind of debate many times before, he knows the delegates will be ready for an agreement after they've exhausted themselves—and not before.

He waves over to his desk one of the young messengers standing against the wall.

"Do you know Mr. Dunlap, the printer?" he asks.

"Yes, sir."

"Run and tell him to get his press ready," he says, putting a small coin in the boy's hand.

He's happy that at the age of seventy he has become a little deaf. In his opinion, the document that his colleagues are trying to make perfect will be read the same way in London no matter how it's written. King George's advisers will tell him that everyone who signed it must hang.

JOIN, OR DIE

Franklin is seventy years old. Just a few months earlier, halfway through a grueling winter journey to Canada and suffering from a variety of illnesses, he sat at a tiny desk pushed close to the fireplace of his drafty hotel room and began a letter: "I have undertaken a fatigue that in my time of life may prove too much for me. So I sit down to write a few friends by way of farewell."

By then, the protests against Britain had turned into war. Franklin was traveling to Canada to persuade its citizens to join the rebellion. He barely completed the trip. It was unsuccessful, which left him feeling even worse. Back in Philadelphia, he had to rest at home for several weeks and couldn't take his place in Congress.

It was difficult for him to make it here this morning; but witnessing this debate, even with its occasional silliness, is good medicine. He believes the work of this

During his trip to Canada, Franklin bought the fur cap that became one of his symbols.

Congress could be the most important moment of his life. The previous summer, an assembly like this one formed the Continental Army out of local militias and made George Washington its commander. Yet colonists still haven't agreed on what they want from this rebellion. Their mood has been changing rapidly. What began as a rebellion against harsh laws has turned into a feeling that all ties with Britain should be cut.

Twenty years earlier Franklin had commissioned what is said to be the first political cartoon in America, a call to the colonies for unity. Each section of the snake represents a colony.

Franklin's opinions have changed in the same way. He once believed the colonies could be united and at the same time remain part of the British Empire. He doesn't belive that anymore. Britain's reaction to the Boston Tea Party was to punish the colonists with strict laws. The colonists called those laws the Intolerable Acts. Now nothing less than independence will satisfy the colonists, including Franklin. Everyone in America seems to be reading and talking about a pamphlet called *Common Sense*, published in Philadelphia this past January. Its anonymous author declares, "no truly natural or religious reason can be assigned" for a society ruled by a king. "All men being originally equals, no one by birth could have a right to set up his own family in perpetual preference to all others forever."

Many people believe the anonymous author is Franklin. He isn't, but he did have a hand in the pamphlet's creation.

A "NATURAL RIGHT"

Two years earlier, as a ship from London docks in Philadelphia, the first mate shouts to the longshoremen on the pier to find a doctor. Bad drinking water has caused an outbreak of typhoid fever. Five passengers are already dead.

By the time the doctor gets to the pier, the crew has helped several sick people off the ship. The doctor examines them right on the pier, giving instructions to the crew and the longshoremen.

"Is that everyone?" the doctor asks the first mate as the last patient is helped away.

"One more aboard. Couldn't leave his cabin. Dead by now, I'd guess."

The doctor goes aboard. Below deck, a man lying on a narrow bunk is not quite dead but nearly so.

"Your name?" the doctor asks.

"Thomas. Thomas Paine." The man is too weak to say more. He points at a shelf above his head on which sits a small leather case. Inside the case the doctor finds several letters addressed in handwriting he thinks he recognizes.

"Are these from Benjamin Franklin?"

The man nods.

The doctor turns to the first mate. "Go tell the longshoremen to fetch my stretcher. I'll care for him at my home."

The man being given special treatment upon arrival in America had left Britain a bankrupt, unemployable failure. But when they met in London, Franklin recognized immediately that Thomas Paine was also a passionate and intelligent essayist whose political ideas would be well received in America. On Franklin's advice and with letters of introduction from him, including one that asked Franklin's son-in-law to give Paine a job, Paine sailed for Philadelphia.

Franklin's doctor friend treats Paine for several weeks, and Paine recovers. By then, several of Franklin's friends have learned about Paine from Franklin and give him work as a tutor for their children. Another friend of Franklin's, a printer with a political magazine, publishes Paine's essays. Then, in early 1776, *Common Sense* is published.

The pamphlet quickly sells an astonishing 100,000 copies. Paine's clear language drives home a simple idea: "A government of our own is our natural right." By that he means more than just a government based in America. He means a government chosen by the American people.

MAD HATTERS

In the past months, cautious politicians have become bolder because they've seen the popularity of Paine's ideas. Today, Congress is voting to adopt a formal Declaration of Independence. That is, they'll vote as soon as they stop talking.

Although Franklin is on the committee that was

appointed by Congress to write the declaration, Thomas Jefferson has done the difficult work of preparing the first draft. About a week ago Jefferson sent the document to Franklin's home, asking Franklin to please review it. Franklin, still confined to his sickbed,

Thomas Paine

smiled as he read Jefferson's words. He made very few changes. Now, however, speaker after speaker at the convention demands trivial amendments.

Franklin notices that Jefferson, who's sitting next to him, winces each time a new change is demanded.

"It appears I've chosen some unlucky expressions," Jefferson whispers.

With the smile of an old man who has seen it all before, Franklin puts a hand on Jefferson's shoulder. "I have made it a rule," he says quietly, "whenever in my power, to avoid becoming the author of papers that will be reviewed by a public body. I took my lesson from an incident which I will relate to you.

"When I was a printer, one of my friends, an apprentice hatter, was about to open shop for himself. His first concern was to have a sign. He composed it in these words 'John Thompson, Hatter, makes and sells hats for ready money,' with a picture of a hat on it. Then he showed it to his friends for their advice.

"The first he showed it to thought the word 'Hatter' repetitive, because it was followed by the words 'makes hats' which showed he was a Hatter. It was struck out.

"The next observed that the word 'makes' might as well be omitted, because his customers would not care who made the hats. If the hats were good and to their liking, people would buy them whoever made them. He struck it out.

"A third friend said he thought the words 'for

ready money' were useless as it was not the custom of the place to sell on credit. Everyone who purchased expected to pay cash. Those words were cut, and the inscription now stood 'John Thompson sells hats.'

"'Sells hats'?! says his next friend. Why, nobody will expect you to give them away. What's the use of that word 'sells'? It was struck out, and 'hats' followed it, because there was one painted on the board.

"So his inscription was reduced ultimately to 'John Thompson' with the figure of a hat!"

While Franklin is telling the story, the last changes are settled. The room is solemn while a clerk reads the final text into the record:

> *When in the course of human events, it becomes necessary for one people to dissolve the political bands which have connected them with another, and to assume among the powers of the earth, the separate and equal station to which the laws of nature and of nature's God entitle them, a decent*

respect to the opinions of mankind requires that they should declare the causes which impel them to the separation.

We hold these truths to be self-evident, that all men are created equal, that they are endowed by their Creator with certain unalienable rights, that among these are life, liberty and the pursuit of happiness.

That to secure these rights, governments are instituted among men, deriving their just powers from the consent of the governed. . . .

We, therefore . . . solemnly publish and declare, That these United Colonies are, and of right ought to be free and independent states; that they are absolved from all allegiance to the British Crown, and that all political connection between them and the state of Great Britain, is and ought to be totally dissolved. . . .

And for the support of this declaration, with a firm reliance on the protection of divine provi-

dence, we mutually pledge to each other our lives,

our fortunes and our sacred honor.

There's the idea that Franklin has been fighting for his whole life: Governments derive their just powers from the consent of the governed. A government that does not come from the people has no right to govern the people.

A little later Congress ends the day's session. A carriage is waiting outside to help Franklin travel the short distance to his home.

"I'll walk today," he tells the driver. He strides off. ⑧

DAY NINE 9

ONE TWO THREE FOUR FIVE SIX

MARCH 20, 1778

KING VS. KING

Paris. 8:32 A.M.

Franklin tugs at the powdered wig he was told to wear today. It doesn't fit and he feels ridiculous. He's tempted to wear the fur hunting cap that has become his trademark since arriving in France a little more than a year ago. The French think it's bizarre, but they admire his bravery for wearing it to stylish occasions. Wig makers have copied it and now some ladies wear what they call *coiffure à la Franklin*—"a Franklin hairstyle." Instead he just pulls off the wig and brushes back what hair he has left on his seventy-two-year-old head. *Let the king see what an American looks like,* he thinks.

AMBASSADOR EXTRAORDINARY

F ranklin has come to France to win its help for the thirteen colonies. Without a foreign ally, the colonies will lose the war with Great Britain. He needs a king to topple a king.

Up until a few months ago, it looked like the British had already won. British troops had captured New York. They'd taken Philadelphia, too, and even occupied Franklin's house there. France has been slow to support the colonies because it doesn't want to side with the losers. The French government is also worried about the idea of democracy. Some of the king's advisers think a country run by commoners will fall apart. They believe only an elite can rule.

Franklin arrived without a clear plan. The government of France, which had assumed the American would be simple to manipulate, can't figure him out. "I really do not know what Franklin has come to do here," says the foreign minister, Count Vergennes.

With no facts to report, people imagine all sorts of things, even secret weapons: Franklin will use mirrors to aim the sun at British ships and set them on fire; Franklin will send a bolt of electricity over the water of the English Channel to shock the whole country; Franklin is building a machine to create earthquakes with electricity, and another to create storms at sea.

In time, Franklin himself becomes the secret weapon. He was already a celebrity when he arrived; now he's a superstar. The French people consider him a scientific and philosophical genius. His portrait is everywhere: hanging on walls in private homes; stamped onto medallions and souvenirs; turned into small statues. Anything that could have a picture of him does, including chamber pots.

He seems to play more than he works, which makes him the perfect diplomat for this mission. In France, a diplomat who tries too hard is ignored. Franklin enjoys mingling in the lighthearted atmosphere of French high society. He tells jokes. He flirts harmlessly. He writes little essays to amuse his friends. In one, written as if it were a scientific paper

Franklin pictured with symbols of his scientific accomplishments: lightning outside the window, and an electrical apparatus to the left.

addressed to the Royal Academy of Brussels, he suggests that, in "this enlightened age," surely someone could discover a medicine to make farts smell as good as perfume.

Along the way, he's winning supporters for America from all parts of French society. The upper class is charmed. The rest of the country admires him deeply. "It is a common observation here," he tells a friend, "that our cause is the cause of all mankind, and that we are fighting for their liberty in defending our own."

SMOKE AND MIRRORS

pies are everywhere. Two of Franklin's colleagues consider themselves his political enemies. (Franklin doesn't feel that way about them. He thinks they're silly, and he's right.) Another is using inside information to make money on the London stock market. A secretary in his office is a secret agent for Britain, reporting back to London every move the Americans make, writing reports in invisible ink and leaving them each week in a secret spot in a park. The French are spying on everyone.

Ignoring these pests as much as possible, Franklin focuses his attention on the French foreign minister, Vergennes. He knows Vergennes wants to hurt Britain by helping the colonists. Even before Franklin arrived, Vergennes was pushing the king toward an alliance. "England is the natural enemy of France," he said. "She is an avid enemy, ambitious, unjust, brimming with bad faith."

Franklin's big chance comes when surprising news arrives from America. The Americans have won a decisive battle at Saratoga, in upstate New York. A large portion of the British army has been captured. Its commander has become a prisoner.

Franklin acts quickly. First, he makes sure the news is printed and spread throughout Paris. Then he uses a little trickery to manipulate the spies.

He lets them report to their bosses that he's planning to sign a peace treaty with England. The spymasters in Britain are delighted. They think Franklin has decided against an alliance with France. When Vergennes hears the same rumor, he's frightened. He doesn't want America to make a peace agreement with Britain that leaves France with nothing. He wants France to share in the trading rights and land that will be part of the peace treaty.

Vergennes rushes to make the alliance, which is what Franklin really wants. The deal is a good one for the Americans. They'll get the money, military aid, and recognition they need.

On the day he signs the agreement, Franklin wears an old coat his colleagues haven't seen before. When asked, he admits why he chose it. It's what he was wearing the day he was viciously condemned in the Cockpit over the Hutchinson letters.

"I want to give this occasion a little revenge," he says.

Palace of Versailles. 10:09 A.M.

crowd lines both sides of the road to the palace gates. The people cry *"Vive Franklin!"*—Long live Franklin!—as his carriage approaches. Franklin notices how obediently they move when guards swing open the large gate, decorated with the royal coat of arms in shining gold. Franklin is disgusted by the waste of France's wealth on royal trimmings, but today's not the day to complain.

The carriage is approached by men who rent ceremonial swords to visitors. It's part of the required dress for the palace. Though Franklin's colleagues oblige, he refuses. There's a moment of muttering among the guards, but it turns out they're also fans of Franklin's. For him, the rule is ignored. They shoo away the men with the swords and send Franklin through—after first breaking their own regulations and shaking his hand.

The elite of France has gathered today. The crowd fills the palace's courtyards. Inside, guests are lined all the way up the staircase to the king's chamber. Some are ambassadors who have refused to meet Franklin because America is not officially a country.

The guests whisper a little too loudly, assuming the Americans can't understand them. They can't get over Franklin's plain brown suit and his lack of a wig. Everyone else is dressed in his or her finest clothes. The men wear medals. The women wear diamonds. Everyone seems to have some insignia or badge or colorful sash to display his or her social rank. Everyone but Franklin, of course.

"Is that what a Quaker wears?" one asks. In France, Franklin is often assumed to be a Quaker.

"He looks like a farmer!"

At exactly noon, the heavy double doors to the king's chamber open.

"The ambassador of the thirteen United Provinces of North America," announces the palace guard.

The thirteen United Provinces. For the first time, Franklin is no longer the representative of colonies. He's the ambassador of a country.

Like Franklin, King Louis XVI wears simple clothes and no wig. In the king's case, it's because he's made little preparation for this meeting. Some diplomats would be offended by the lack of ceremony. Franklin is pleased and relieved.

"Please assure the Congress of my friendship," Louis XVI says. "I hope this will be for the good of the two nations."

Franklin at the Palace of Versailles

"Your Majesty can count on the gratitude of the Congress," Franklin replies. He flatters the king with a comparison to Great Britain's King George III: "If all monarchies were governed by the principles which are in your heart, Sire, republics would never be formed." That's not what he always believes, but it sounds good today.

ANY REGRETS, LOUIS?: IN 1789, THE FRENCH PEOPLE, PARTLY INSPIRED BY AMERICA, PUT AN END TO THEIR MONARCHY. LOUIS XVI AND HIS WIFE, MARIE ANTOINETTE, WERE EXECUTED IN 1793.

As soon as Franklin steps out of the king's chamber, Franklin senses the difference in the mood of the other guests. Thanks to the king, America is now officially a country in their eyes.

That evening Franklin and his colleagues are guests of honor at a grand diplomatic dinner. Franklin sits where the British ambassador would normally sit. The ambassador and his wife are at home, packing. They're leaving France tomorrow, outsmarted. ⑨

DAY 10

TEN

SEPTEMBER 17, 1787

A RISING SUN

Philadelphia. 10:59 A.M.

Guards are blocking the doors of the Philadelphia statehouse. The windows are nailed shut. No spies will hear the meetings taking place inside.

For four months, through a hot, humid summer, most of the best minds in America have gathered for secret debates over a plan to bring the thirteen newly independent states into a single union. Today is the final debate, the day on which the plan will be put to a vote. There's been a lot of arguing, and even the man who proposed many parts of the plan, Edmund Randolph, of Virginia, doesn't want to vote for the final version. He doesn't believe Virginians will like it.

Some of the most famous names of the Revolutionary War are refusing to take part. Samuel Adams, of Boston, explains to his friends that he fears "a national government instead of a federal union of sovereign states." Patrick Henry, of Virginia, is more blunt. "I smelt a rat . . . tending toward the monarchy," he says. Alexander Hamilton takes part for a while, but then returns to New York.

A BUMPY RIDE

The thirteen states that were once allied against a common enemy have been bickering among themselves since the British surrendered six years earlier. Their distrust of one another now threatens to reduce North America to an uneasy collection of small, unfriendly countries. France, Spain, and even Great Britain are ready to form new alliances that will give them control of the states and of the American frontier.

Of the fifty-five delegates, Franklin is by far the oldest at eighty-one. His health is not good. On the day the convention opened he was too sick to come. Later, he was carried from his home to the meetings in a sedan chair—like a carriage without wheels, held

Franklin in his sedan chair

aloft by four men. The bumpy ride of a carriage would have been too uncomfortable.

Then, as this summer wore on, his energies grew. Some of the delegates are exhausted, others are bored, and a few are angry at the direction of the discussions; Franklin, however, is offering ideas with more enthusiasm than most of the younger men possess. The other delegates don't always understand his plans, but their respect for him is deep.

Only George Washington, who is presiding over the convention, commands a similar moral authority. Washington is quiet through most of the discussions. He's not there to argue for one plan or another. His contribution is his character: All the delegates know that he demands the highest degree of civility from himself and from others. These fiery rebels, who have taken on the British Empire and declared themselves independent of the most powerful king in the world, are afraid to misbehave in front of the serious, courageous hero of the Revolutionary war.

Even today, with the future of America at stake, and with so much disagreement that a vote in favor of this new Constitution seems unlikely to pass, it will fall to Franklin to bring the delegates together.

IMPERFECT UNION

It's easy now to look on the Philadelphia Convention and see the wisdom of voting in favor of the Constitution. Back then, the future was not so clear. The original document didn't include many of the rights and freedoms considered part of the American identity. Freedom of speech, freedom of religion, freedom of assembly, freedom of the press—all these were added later. The Constitution didn't resolve the differences over slavery that would eventually lead to the Civil War.

Samuel Adams and Patrick Henry aren't staying away from the convention because they dislike the idea of individual freedom. Like others, they fear a new federal government with power over state governments will weaken the individual liberties many of the states have made into law. Patrick Henry's concern about a monarchy is reasonable. There was talk of a lifetime appointment for the head of state.

But the need for some sort of union is obvious. Conflicts between the states are growing. New York tries to raise money by demanding a fee from any ship

The State House in Philadelphia

landing from New Jersey across the Hudson River. New Jersey fights back with a tax of its own. Maryland and Virginia can't agree on their border. Several states want to expand westward. There are arguments about paying debts left from the Revolutionary War.

Up to this time, the states had operated under a weak constitution, the Articles of Confederation, written in 1777. There was a single idea behind that constitution, and it was a simple one: Work together to defeat the British. The federal government looked nothing like the federal government of modern times. There was only one house of Congress, with no division between senators and representatives; there was no presidency in charge of putting Congress's laws into action; there was no federal court system. Congress could not even pass a tax law to pay for the war. It had to go to the individual states for money.

In 1786, when Maryland and Virginia met to settle their border dispute, representatives of some other states attended, hoping a broader solution might

appear. The delegates knew that a stronger constitution would be controversial and that some states
would object to it. They said, however, the "embar-
rassments" of the current problems were "of a nature
so serious, as, in the view of your commissioners to
render the situation of the United States delicate and
critical, calling for an exertion of the united virtue
and wisdom of all the members."

The following summer, the Philadelphia convention began.

GIVE AND TAKE

arlier in the summer, Franklin makes
several proposals to the convention. All
are refused. He proposes a single elected
assembly; there are two. He suggests that a council
lead the executive branch of the government; instead
there will be a chief executive, the president of the

United States. He recommends that members of Congress serve for free; instead, they'll be allowed to set their own pay.

Now Franklin simply hopes to bring together the many unhappy delegates.

Some of the difficulties have existed since the beginning of time. Small states fear big states. Farmers distrust bankers. Each state has tenaciously guarded its self-interest.

Some of the issues reflect the era. Many delegates question the wisdom of democracy. They associate it with mobs. They believe only men with a certain level of wealth should be allowed to vote.

The most difficult issue has been the formula for representation. Should every American be counted equally? If so, then states with large populations would always dominate the new assembly. Should each state be given a single vote instead? Then smaller states could establish laws that the majority of Americans have voted against.

A delegate from Connecticut, Roger Sherman, had proposed a combination of the two methods. A House of Representatives would be based on population, and a Senate would give each state a vote equal to the other states. His proposal was rejected earlier in the summer. Franklin recently proposed it again, sensing that the delegates might be ready for it, having refused every other choice. This time it's accepted.

In an odd twist, it's the Northern, anti-slavery states that won't allow slaves to be counted in the general population. They want to weaken the slave states to end slavery sooner. In another compromise, it's agreed to count each slave as "three fifths" of a person. Although this language is insulting, it does weaken the slave states.

Slavery itself has been debated extensively. In simplest terms, the Northern states would like to see it abolished, and the Southern states are prepared to leave the Union if that happens. But there have been some surprising moments in the debates. George

Mason, a delegate from Virginia, made one of the most passionate speeches against slavery:

> Every master of slaves is born a petty tyrant. [Slaves] bring the judgment of heaven on a country. As nations cannot be rewarded or punished in the next world they must be in this. By an inevitable chain of causes and effects, providence punishes national sins by national calamities. I hold it essential to every point of view that the general [federal] government should have power to prevent the increase of slavery.

Some of the Northern delegates believe it's not necessary to force the issue right now. They say slavery seems to be disappearing naturally. There's a sense among the delegates that it will be gone entirely within twenty years, thanks to growing public sentiment against it and increased immigration of European workers.

The delegates recently reached a compromise. By an eight to four vote, the states decided that the new federal government will not be allowed to ban the slave trade before 1808. They've also established the right to tax slave owners for newly arriving slaves. Some delegates hope that by adding this expense, Congress will hinder the slave trade. Others point out that the tax gives the federal government profit from slavery.

Some delegates sense that these compromises on slavery will not resolve the issue. A few believe slavery will eventually break the union. At least one admits to his concern about a "civil war" arising from the various conflicts already occurring between the states.

None of them imagine that a little more than seventy years in the future, one of the bloodiest wars in history will be fought to finally decide the constitutional issues they have not been able to settle peacefully this summer.

ALWAYS IN THE RIGHT

hen the delegates have settled in their places, the final draft of the Constitution is read aloud. As soon as it's done, Franklin catches George Washington's eye. Washington nods to him, and in a commanding voice announces, "The chair recognizes Dr. Franklin."

Franklin pushes himself up from his chair unsteadily. Watching him most closely is James Wilson, another delegate from Pennsylvania, who has shaped much of the final document the delegates are now considering.

Franklin sees on the faces of many delegates that they're uneasy with this Constitution. Franklin knows they're worried about the reactions of citizens back in their respective home states when the document is made public. None of them has been able to wholly satisfy the people back home, and they don't want their reputations to suffer. They've created a federal government with power over state governments in many areas of law, yet they have not listed the rights and freedoms for which Americans have just fought a war. Their formula for votes in Congress, intended to give every state something that would make it happy, has of course left every state feeling that the others have an advantage. Some of the delegates believe this convention will look like a failure.

Franklin understands the delegates are afraid of taking a leap of faith that he believes is necessary and right. This fear is what he needs to address.

Unfortunately, he can't.

After a summer in this overheated room, he's too ill. He doesn't have the physical strength to make the speech he wants to give.

Knowing this, he sets aside pride and arranges with Washington to have someone speak for him. Washington is eager for the delegates to hear Franklin's words in any way possible.

"If you'll allow me," Franklin says to the delegates,

"I have some thoughts to offer before we vote on this Constitution. Mr. Wilson has kindly offered to read them for me."

Wilson rises and clears his throat; then, with a nod to Franklin, he begins:

I confess that there are several parts of this Constitution which I do not at present approve, but I am not sure I shall never approve them. For, having lived long, I have experienced many instances of being obliged, by better information or fuller consideration, to change opinions, even on important subjects, which I once thought right, but found to be otherwise. It is therefore that, the older I grow, the more apt I am to doubt my own judgment, and to pay more respect to the judgment of others. Most men, indeed, as well as most sects in religion, think themselves in possession of all truth, and that wherever others differ from them, it is so far error. Steele, a Protestant, in a dedication, tells the Pope, that the only difference between our churches, in their opinions of the certainty of their doctrines, is, "the Church of Rome is infallible, and the Church of England is never in the wrong." But though many private persons think almost as highly of their own infallibility as of that of their sect, few express it so naturally as a certain French lady, who, in a dispute with her sister, said, "I don't know how it happens, sister, but I meet with nobody but myself that is always in the right."

In these sentiments, sir, I agree to this Constitution, with all its faults, if they are such; because I think a general government necessary for us, and there is no form of government, but what may be a blessing to the people if well administered; and believe further, that this is likely to be well administered for a course of years. . . .

Thus I consent, sir, to this Constitution, because I expect no better, and because I am not sure, that *it is not the best. . . . On the whole, sir, I cannot*

help expressing a wish that every member of the

Convention, who may still have objections to it,

would with me, on this occasion, doubt a little of

his own infallibility, and, to make manifest our

unanimity, put his name to this instrument.

The speech works—almost. Franklin hoped it would convince every delegate to sign. He very much wants unanimous agreement. But after a few more minutes of discussion, it's clear three delegates won't sign. They still believe the compromises, rather than giving every state a reason to agree to the document, will instead give each state a reason to reject it.

Washington calls for the signatures of the delegates who will agree. As they gather around Washington's desk for the formal signing, Franklin can't resist a final comment.

Pointing to the back of Washington's chair, which is decorated with a painting of the sun, he says, "I was once told that painters have difficulty showing the difference between a rising and a setting sun. I have often, in the course of this session, as my hopes and fears rose and fell, looked at this design without being able to tell if it was rising or setting. But now, at length, I have the happiness to know it is a rising, and not a setting sun." **10**

The opening of the Constitution. The preamble confirms the
idea that common citizens are meant to govern themselves: "We
the people of the United States, in order to form a more perfect
union, establish justice, insure domestic tranquility, provide for
the common defence, promote the general welfare, and secure the
blessings of liberty to ourselves and our posterity, do ordain and
establish this Constitution for the United States of America."

① ② ③ ④ ⑤ ⑥ ⑦

⑧ ⑨ → ⑩ ← 1 2 3

4 5 6 7 8 9 10 1 2

3 4 5 6 7 8 9 10 **12**

3 4 5 6 7 8 9 10

ONE TWO THREE FOUR FIVE SIX

AFTERWORD

———◆———

DECEMBER 15,
1791

A NEW EDITION

Richmond, Virginia.

n April 17, 1790, in his bed in Philadelphia, Franklin dies. He is eight-four years old. Sixty-two years earlier, as a young man, he had written and published an epitaph for himself that has already been reprinted countless times in America and throughout Europe.

The body of

B. Franklin, Printer;

Like the cover of an old book,

Its contents worn out,

and stripped of its lettering and gilding

Lies here, food for worms.

But the work shall not be wholly lost:

For it will, as he believed, appear once more,

In a new and more perfect edition,

Corrected and amended

By the Author.

Today in Virginia, a year and a half after his death, what may be his greatest achievement, the Constitution of the United States, will appear in a new and more elegant edition, revised and corrected. Virginia will become the tenth state to vote in favor of the Bill of Rights, ten amendments to the Constitution that guarantee individual liberties. Some of the most patriotic Founding Fathers fought against the Constitution because it did not include these rights. Franklin believed the Constitution gives the American people the chance to improve the country one step at a time.

Before the vote, a clerk reads the list of amendments to the legislators:

> . . . Congress shall make no law respecting an establishment of religion, or prohibiting the free exercise thereof; or abridging the freedom of speech, or of the press; or the right of the people peaceably to assemble, and to petition the government for a redress of grievances.

> . . . A well regulated militia, being necessary to the security of a free state, the right of the people to keep and bear arms, shall not be infringed.

> . . . No soldier shall, in time of peace be quartered in any house, without the consent of the owner . . .

> . . . The right of the people to be secure in their persons, houses, papers, and effects, against unreasonable searches and seizures, shall not be violated, and no warrants shall issue, but upon

probable cause, supported by oath or affirmation, and particularly describing the place to be searched, and the persons or things to be seized.

. . . No person shall be held to answer for any capital, or otherwise infamous crime, unless on a presentment or indictment of a grand jury, except in cases arising in the land or naval forces, or in the militia, when in actual service in time of war or public danger; nor shall any person be subject for the same offence to be twice put in jeopardy of life or limb; nor shall be compelled in any criminal case to be a witness against himself, nor be deprived of life, liberty, or property, without due process of law; nor shall private property be taken for public use, without just compensation.

. . . In all criminal prosecutions, the accused shall enjoy the right to a speedy and public trial, by an impartial jury of the state and district wherein the crime shall have been committed . . . and to be informed of the nature and cause of the accusation;

*to be confronted with the witnesses against him;
to have compulsory process for obtaining witnesses
in his favor, and to have the assistance of counsel
for his defense.*

*. . . In suits at common law, where the value in
controversy shall exceed twenty dollars, the right
of trial by jury shall be preserved. . . .*

*. . . Excessive bail shall not be required, nor
excessive fines imposed, nor cruel and unusual
punishments inflicted.*

*. . . The enumeration in the Constitution, of
certain rights, shall not be construed to deny or
disparage others retained by the people.*

*The powers not delegated to the United States
by the Constitution, nor prohibited by it to the
states, are reserved to the states respectively, or to
the people.*

The vote is taken. The legislators agree. The amendments are now law throughout America.

These amendments don't make the Constitution perfect. On this day, the Constitution still allows slavery. It doesn't give voting rights to women. It doesn't prevent individual states from making it difficult or impossible for other people to vote. Many lives will be sacrificed before those rights and freedoms are added.

Still, Franklin's faith in the founding idea of America, and his role in making that possible, has been justified today in a lasting way. A government created by the people being governed—or as many of them as the limited opinions of the times allow—has taken a great step toward resolving its disputes reasonably and peacefully. In an era when common people are considered unfit to govern themselves, the United States, for all its faults, is setting an example that countries all over the world will soon follow, overthrowing monarchs and dictators. Despite missteps in the centuries since, that legacy continues. ⟶

NOTES AND SELECTED
BIBLIOGRAPHY

All noteworthy dialogue and speeches are closely based on the
historical record, which includes Franklin's recollections in letters and
his autobiography. Some allowance has been made for archaic words,
spelling, and grammar.

Brands, H.W. *The First American: The Life and Times of Benjamin Franklin*. New York:
    Doubleday, 2000.
Cook, Don. *The Long Fuse: How England Lost the American Colonies, 1760–1785*.
    New York: The Atlantic Monthly Press, 1995.
Franklin, Benjamin. *Benjamin Franklin, His Autobiography, 1706–1757*. New York:
    Bartleby.com, 2001. Online at http://www.bartleby.com/1/1/
Isaacson, Walter. *Benjamin Franklin: An American Life*. New York: Simon & Schuster, 2003.
Jennings, Francis. *Benjamin Franklin, Politician*. New York: W. W. Norton, 1996.
Morgan, Edmund S. *Benjamin Franklin*. New Haven: Yale University Press, 2002.
Van Doren, Carl. Benjamin Franklin. New York: Viking Press, 1938.

page 51: Quoted in Van Doren, 159. See also online:
    http://www.rarebookroom.org/Control/frkelc/index.html
page 55: "Nothing, perhaps": Adams, C.F. (ed.), *The Works of John Adams*. Boston,
    Little, Brown, 1856. Vol. 1, 660.
page 65: "he received me," and conversation between Franklin and Penn: Cook,
    40–41 and Brands, 301–302.
pages 73–84: Stamp Act testimony and reactions: Cook, 51–69.
pages 91–94: "one of the nastiest" and Wedderburn accusations: Cook, 182–184.
page 97: "As a result of this humiliation": Cook, 186.
page 107: "It appears": Hazelton, John. *The Declaration of Independence: Its History*.
    New York: 1906; quoted in Colbert, David. *Eyewitness to America*. New York:
    Pantheon Books, 1997. 81.
page 117: "It is a common observation": Isaacson, 339.
page 118: "England is the natural enemy": Isaacson, 337.
pages 120–123: Versailles scene: "Memoir of Jonathan Loring Austin," *Boston
    Monthly Magazine*, July 1826; René de La Croix, duc de Castries, *La France
    et l'indépendance américaine*. Paris: Perrin, 1975. 187; Armstrong, Annie
    Emma. *Heroes, Philosophers and Courtiers of the Time of Louis XVI*. London:
    Hurst and Blackett, 1863. 197–199.
page 139: "I confess": from James Madison's report of the convention debates.
    Available online: http://www.yale.edu/lawweb/avalon/debates/917.htm